A KNITTER'S GALLERY OF
Mitered Squares
5 Unique Designs in color, texture and lace

Knit Creatively

Jane & Jill

Acknowledgements

There are so many people who helped make this book possible. First, Miss Virginia and Aunt Winnie. These wonderful women taught us to knit. Both are gone now but forever in our hearts.

A pattern with a few eyelet rows in Domino Knitting by Vivian Hoxbro started us thinking just how much we could do with stitch patterns in mitered squares. It would be neglectful not to also pay homage to Virginia Woods Bellamy, the mother of modular knitting.

I (Jill) would never have dreamt that a random roommate assignment at Knitter's Connection would take us from idea to plan in a few days. Laura Farson was more helpful than she will ever know (though we try to tell her just how helpful she was in focusing all our ideas). JC Briar and Andrea Wong very generously shared their experiences and gave us some valuable insights into writing a book.

Molly Bigelow, daughter, sister and graphic designer extraordinaire, took our words and made them pretty. Sarah Peasley, technical editor, corrected the grammar, punctuation and spelling and made sure that we said what we meant to say. This book would have looked very sad without them.

LuAnn Williams did the photographs for Misty Valley. Kyla Williams, Ruby Fultz and Kathy Sentgeorge stood patiently in wool and alpaca on hot summer evenings and rainy mornings until the shots were just right.

Many people reviewed and gave opinions on this book. We especially want to thank Meg Croft and Pat Black for slogging through that very first draft.

A special thank you to Amy Sutley for the many times she boosted our moral by softly saying "You are not trying to do this, you are doing it". She reminded us to trust in ourselves and finish the book which started with the hope of providing knitter's with information and encourage them to trust in their own creative talents

This would not have happened without the constant moral support and encouragement from Gordy and Rick. They never doubted, even when we sometimes were questioning ourselves. Their words of wisdom saved us from giving up. We could not have done this without their love and support.

ISBN 978-0-615-94293-3
Copyright © February 2014
First Edition
Email: info@b-ewe-tiful.com
Website: www.b-ewe-tiful.com
Printed in Canada

BLUE
CABIN
PRESS

Table of Contents

Mitered Square Basics

Mitered squares are created by decreasing 2 stitches in the center of every other row. This creates a square shape with the stitches set at right angles to each other. The center decreasing creates a line stretching diagonally from the cast-on edge to the last live stitch.

The cast-on stitches create 2 sides of the square. Continue knitting until 1 stitch remains. Cut the yarn, elongate the loop, and pull up until the yarn pulls through.

How To Combine The Patterns In This Book

Many of the Squares in this book will work out to the same size, but not all. When combining different square patterns, be sure to first knit samples. Follow the Adapability guideline to adjust the size if necessary.

Cast On

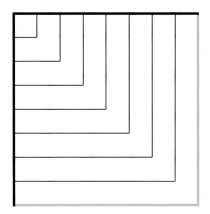

All Sample Squares were made with
Green Mountain Spinnery *Sylvan Spirt.*

Each chart in this book will be read the same way.

1. Worked flat. Odd numbered rows are Wrong Side (WS) rows and even numbered rows are Right Side (RS) rows.

2. The first stitch of every row except Row 1 is slipped as if to knit. This allows for easier pick-up of the stitches for the adjoining squares. The last stitch of every row is purled.

3. The 'No Stitch' symbol is a placeholder in the chart as you decrease the stitches. When a 'No Stitch' symbol is encountered, pretend it is not there and move to the next symbol.

4. The stitch count is correct after the row is completed. For example, in Row 2 of the following chart, there are 35 stitches at the beginning of the row but 33 stitches at the end. This reflects the 2 stitches decreased in that row.

5. At the bottom of the chart page will be a legend. For instructions on how to work a stitch, refer to Glossary.

Adaptability Rating 1, 2 or 3

Many of the squares in this book can be adapted to change the size of the finished square. Under each photo will be an Adaptability Rating of 1, 2 or 3.

Adaptability 1 squares can use any odd number of stitches. They size up and down with ease.

Adaptability 2 squares must be adapted using a certain multiple of stitches.

Adaptability 3 squares are best left alone.

Sample Square Chart

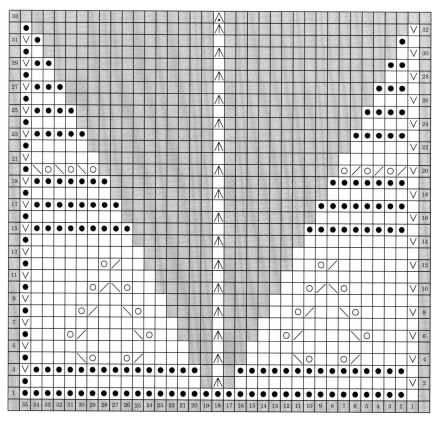

☐ k (RS), p (WS)   ● p (RS), k (WS)   ☑ sl1wyib   ○ yo   ╱ k2tog   ╲ ssk   ⋀ cdd   ⛛ cddp   ▨ no stitch

See pg. 74 for photo of this square.

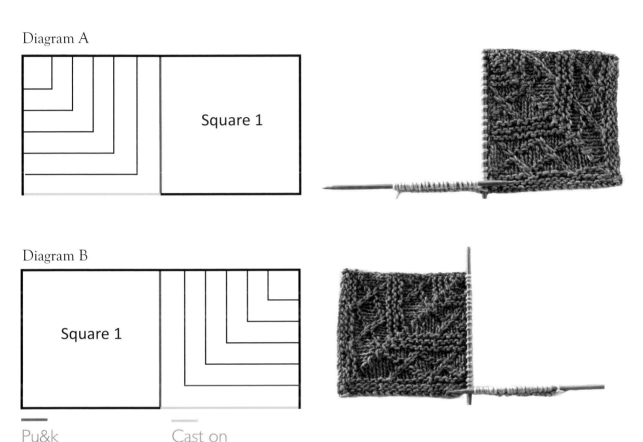

Diagram A

Square 1

Diagram B

Square 1

Pu&k   Cast on

Square 1 can be oriented any way you like. Always pu&k with RS facing. Cast on half of (the total number of stitches -1). Pu&k half of (the total number of stitches +1 for center stitch). Ex. 25-stitch square: cast on 12 stitches and pu&k 13.

Picking up a square on the left (Diagram A) will result in a square with the miter running from bottom right to top left (direction of arrow). Start by pu&k stitches along desired edge of Square 1, then cast on stitches.

Picking up a square on the right (Diagram B) will result in a square with the miter running from bottom left to top right. Start by casting on stitches, then pu&k along desired edge of Square 1.

How To Pick Up and Knit (pu&k)

1. Insert needle into both legs of the slipped stitch (or stitch from cast-on edge).

2. Knit the stitch.

Pick Up a Square On Point

To build squares on point (diamonds), two squares must first be knit separately.

1. Leave the live stitch of Square 1. It will be used in a different square.

2. Pu&k half of (the total number of stitches -1) along the left edge of Square 1.

3. Join Squares 1 and 2 together by pu&k in the loop behind the last cast-on stitch of Square 1 and the first cast-on stitch of Square 2 and knit the 2 together. If there is a square below, knit the live stitch of that square instead. This will be the center stitch.

4. Pu&k half of (the total number of stitches -1) along the right edge of Square 2.

5. Leave live stitch of Square 2. It will be used in a different square.

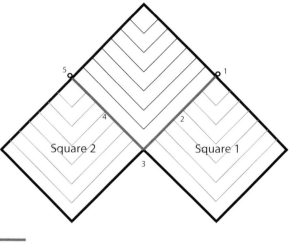

Pu&k

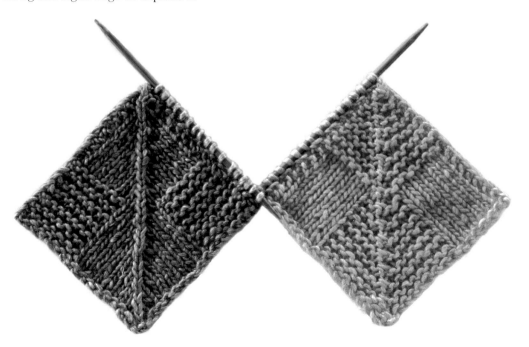

When squares are built on point they become diamonds. Sometimes it is necessary to create partial diamonds or triangles (Diagram 1). Triangles create sraight edges on the top, bottom, left and right. A left triangle (LT) is on the left side of a diamond but is the right half of a square. A right triangle (RT) is on the right side of a diamond but is the left half of a square. A top triangle (TT) is the first half of a diamond.

The left and right triangles are worked at the same time as the diamonds. The top triangles are added at the end. Diagram 2 shows two ways diamonds and triangles are created. Building diagonally (black numbers) allows for fewer ends to weave in as the yarn can be carried from one diamond to the next. If the diamonds are changing color or yarn, the diagonal order is not necessary and diamonds can be created in rows (red numbers).

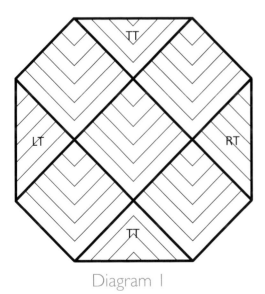

Diagram 1

Diagram 2

Convert Square to Left Triangle

Left triangles are worked on the left side of a diamond as you are looking at it.

1. Remove all stitches to the left of the double decrease symbol on Sample Square Chart (pg. 3). The decreases will be at the end of the RS rows.

2. Replace double decrease (cdd, sl1k2p, cddp, sl1p2p) with a single decease (p2tog).

3. P2tog on last row.

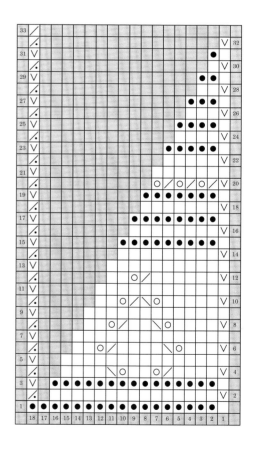

□ k (RS), p (WS)   ● p (RS), k (WS)   ☑ sl1wyib   ○ yo   ⟋ k2tog   ⟍ ssk   ⧄ p2tog   ▨ no stitch

Convert Square to Right Triangle

Right triangles are worked on the right side of a diamond as you are looking at it.

1. Remove all stitches to the right of the double decrease symbol on Sample Square Chart (pg. 3). The decreases will be at the beginning of the RS rows.

2. Replace double decrease (cdd, sl1k2p, cddp, sl1p2p) with a single decease (ssk).

3. Ssp on last row.

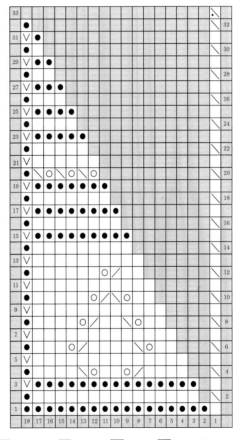

| □ k (RS), p (WS) | ● p (RS), k (WS) | ☑ sl1wyib | ○ yo | ╱ k2tog | ╲ ssk | ⟍ ssp | ▨ no stitch |

Convert Square to Top Triangle

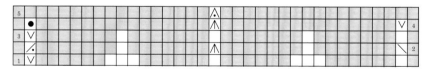

Top triangles are used to fill in the gaps created by placing the mitered squares on point. They are placed at the top and bottom of the piece. Top triangles are the last pieces worked. To work bottom triangles, turn work upside down and work same as top triangles.

1. Work as for full square except ssk at the beginning and p2tog at the end of every RS row.

2. Keep the slipped stitch at the beginning and the p1 at the end of every WS row.

3. When 3 stitches remain, sl1, p2tog, then pass the slipped stitch over the p2tog on the WS row.

The last 2 rows can vary based on the number of stitches in the triangle. Triangles with a multiple of 4 stitches -1 will look like Diagram 1. Triangles with a multiple of 4 stitches +1 will look like Diagram 2.

Diagram 1

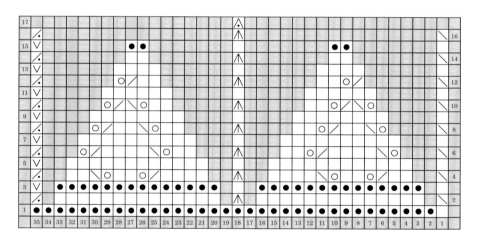

Diagram 2

☐ k (RS), p (WS) ● p (RS), k (WS) ☑ sl1wyib ⊙ yo ⟋ k2tog ⟍ ssk ⟰ cdd ⟰ cddp ☐ no stitch

Stack Squares

Squares can be built upon one another in many directions: right to left, bottom to top, left to right, top to bottom or a combination, even starting with the center square. Here are just a few ways to go, starting with Square 1 at the bottom left. Let your imagination run wild!

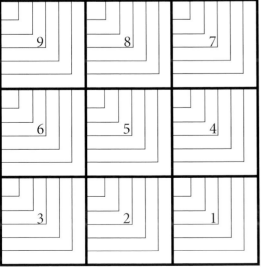

Try a reversible pu&k.

If both sides of the project will be seen, try a reversible pu&k.

Step 1. Pu&k in the back leg of slipped stitch.

Step 2. Pu&k in the front leg of the next slipped stitch.

Repeat these 2 steps until all stitches have been picked up. It doesn't matter which step is last.

Change the amount of stitches to pu&k.

Sometimes the number of pu&k stitches will vary from square to square. For example, building a 37-stitch block onto a 35-stitch block will require 1 extra pu&k on each side.

To pu&k fewer stitches, simply skip a stitch.

To pu&k more stitches, work Steps 1 and 2 above in the same stitch.

Color Square 1

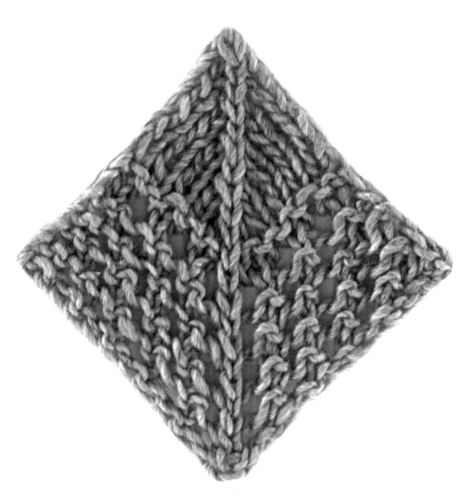

Adaptability 2 Increase or decrease by a multiple of 4 stitches.

Color Square 1

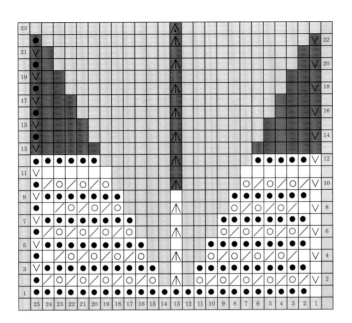

■ color B □ k (RS), p (WS) ● p (RS), k (WS) ∨ sl1wyib

○ yo ╱ k2tog ╲ ssk ⋀ cdd ⋀̇ cddp ▨ no stitch

Color Square 2

Adaptability | Any odd number of stitches can be used.

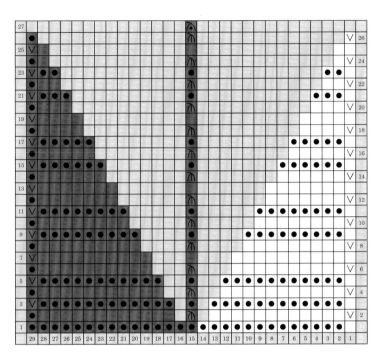

color B ▢ k (RS), p (WS) ● p (RS), k (WS) ⊻ sl1wyib ⋔ sl1k2p ⌂ sl1p2p ▢ no stitch

Color Square 3

Adaptability 1 Any odd number of stitches can be used.

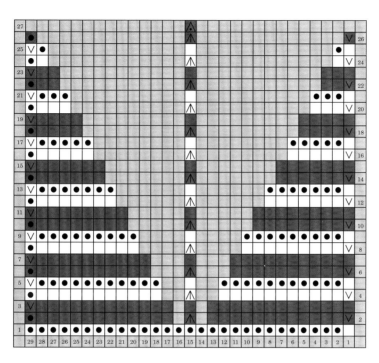

■ color B □ k (RS), p (WS) ● p (RS), k (WS) ⋁ sl1wyib ⋀ cdd ⟁ cddp ▨ no stitch

Color Square 4

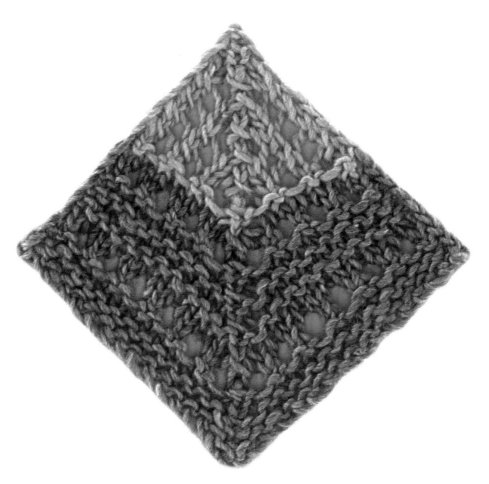

Adaptability 2 Increase or decrease by a multiple of 4 stitches.

Color Square 4

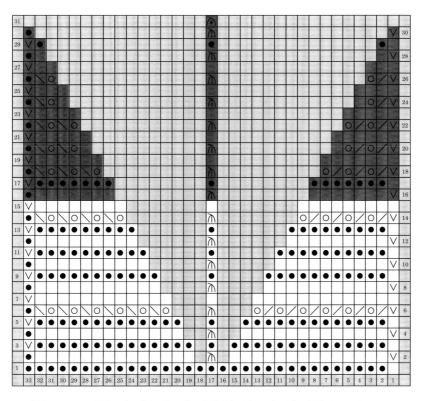

	color B		k (RS), p (WS)	●	p (RS), k (WS)	☑	sl1wyib
○	yo	╱	k2tog	╲	ssk	⋏	sl1k2p	⌒	sl1p2p		no stitch

Color Square 5

Adaptability | Any odd number of stitches can be used.

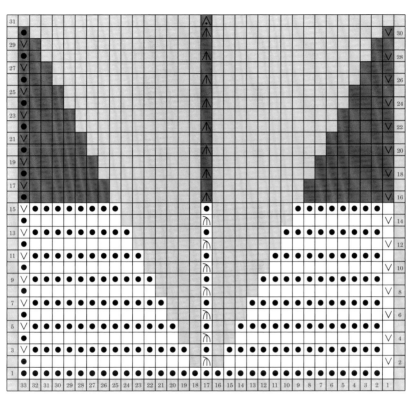

color B ☐ k (RS), p (WS) ● p (RS), k (WS) ∨ sl1wyib ∧ cdd ⅄ sl1k2p △ cddp ☐ no stitch

Color Square 6

Adaptability 2 Increase or decrease by a multiple of 4 stitches.

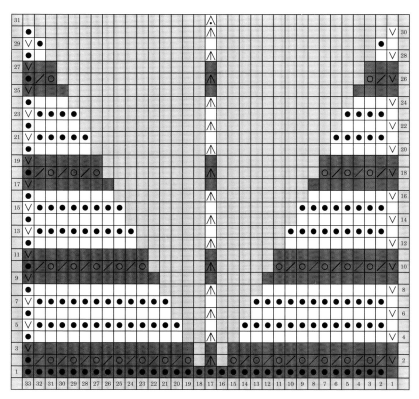

■ color B □ k (RS), p (WS) ● p (RS), k (WS) ⊽ sl1wyib

○ yo ／ k2tog ⋀ cdd ⋀ cddp ▦ no stitch

Color Square 7

Adaptability I Any odd number of stitches can be used.

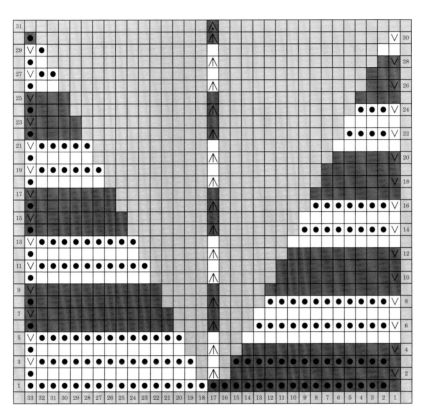

color B ☐ k (RS), p (WS) ● p (RS), k (WS) ⋁ sl1wyib ⋀ cdd ⋀ cddp ☐ no stitch

Color Square 8

Adaptability 2 Increase or decrease by a multiple of 4 stitches.

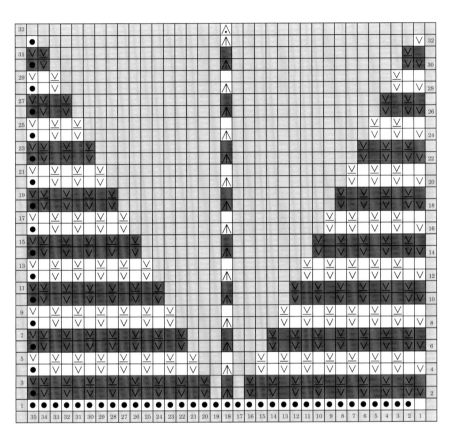

■ color B ☐ k (RS), p (WS) ● p (RS), k (WS) ⩒ sl1wyib ⩔ sl1wyif ⋀ cdd ⩗ cddp ☐ no stitch

Color Square 9

Adaptability 2 Increase or decrease by a multiple of 4 stitches.

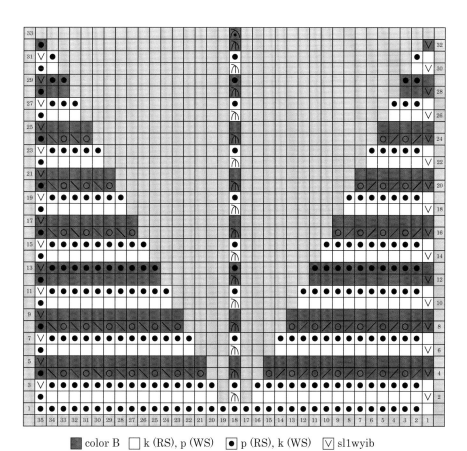

	color B		k (RS), p (WS)		● p (RS), k (WS)		⋁ sl1wyib
○ yo		╱ k2tog		╲ ssk		⋔ sl1k2p	⋔ sl1p2p		no stitch

Color Square 10

Adaptability 3 Best to follow chart exactly.

Color Square 10

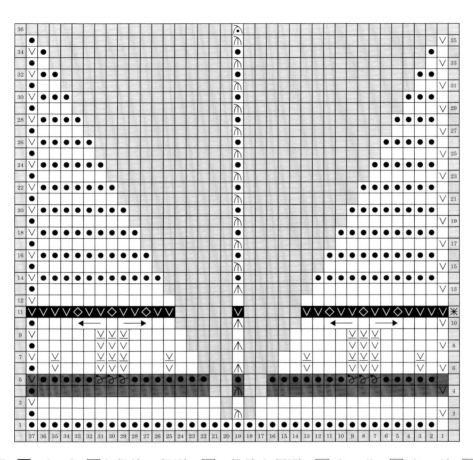

■ color B ■ color C □ k (RS), p (WS) ● p (RS), k (WS) ∨ sl1wyib ⊻ sl1wyif ⌐ pw2x

⋀ cdd ⋀ sl1k2p ⌐ sl1p2p ☐ no stitch ⟶ 1x2rc ⟵ 1x2lc ◇ bobble ✳ be

Color Square 11

Adaptability l Any odd number of stitches can be used.

Color Square 11

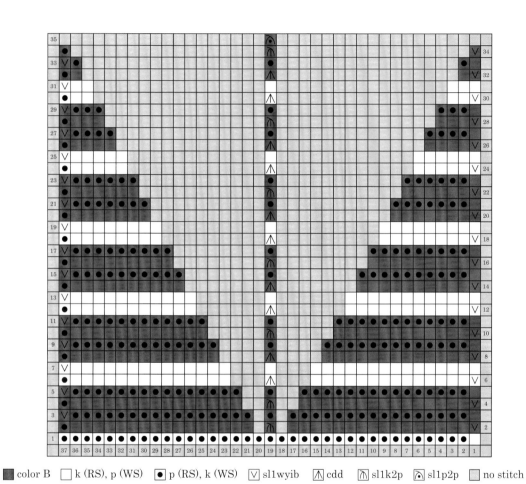

| | color B | | k (RS), p (WS) | • | p (RS), k (WS) | $\vee$ | sl1wyib | $\wedge$ | cdd | $\overline{\wedge}$ | sl1k2p | $\overline{\odot}$ | sl1p2p | | no stitch |

Color Square 12

Adaptability 2 Increase or decrease by a multiple of 4 stitches.

Color Square 12

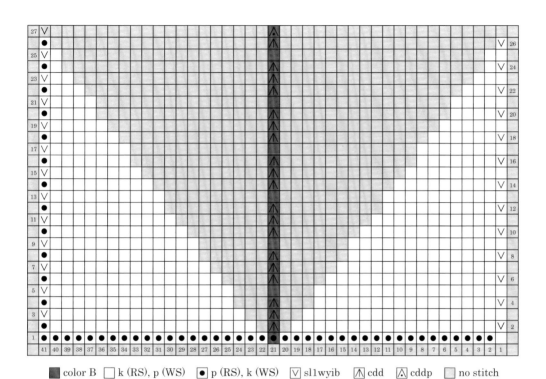

color B ▢ k (RS), p (WS) ● p (RS), k (WS) ⋁ sl1wyib ⋀ cdd ⋀ cddp ▢ no stitch

Color Square 13

Adaptability 2 Increase or decrease by a multiple of 4 stitches.

Color Square 13

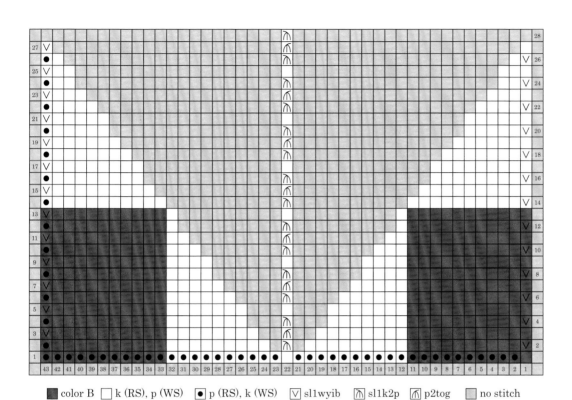

| | color B | | k (RS), p (WS) | | ● | p (RS), k (WS) | | ∨ | sl1wyib | | ⋏ | sl1k2p | | ⋏ | p2tog | | | no stitch |

Color Square 14

Adaptability 2 Increase or decrease by a multiple of 4 stitches.

Color Square 14

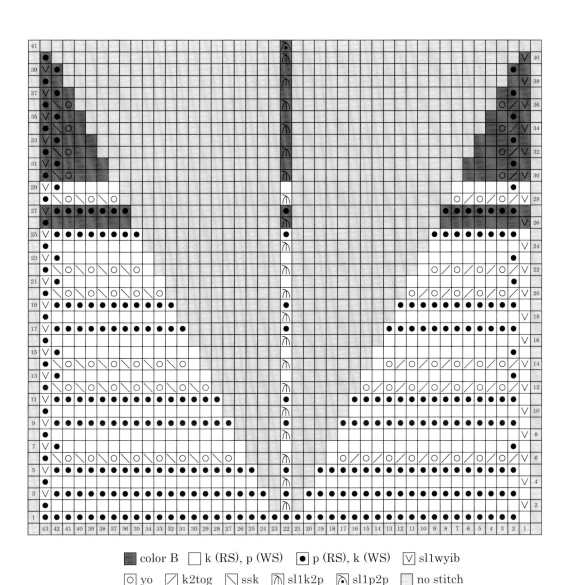

■ color B	□ k (RS), p (WS)	● p (RS), k (WS)	⋁ sl1wyib
◯ yo	╱ k2tog	╲ ssk	⋀ sl1k2p	⋀ sl1p2p	☐ no stitch

Color Square 15

Adaptability 2 Increase or decrease by a multiple of 8 stitches.

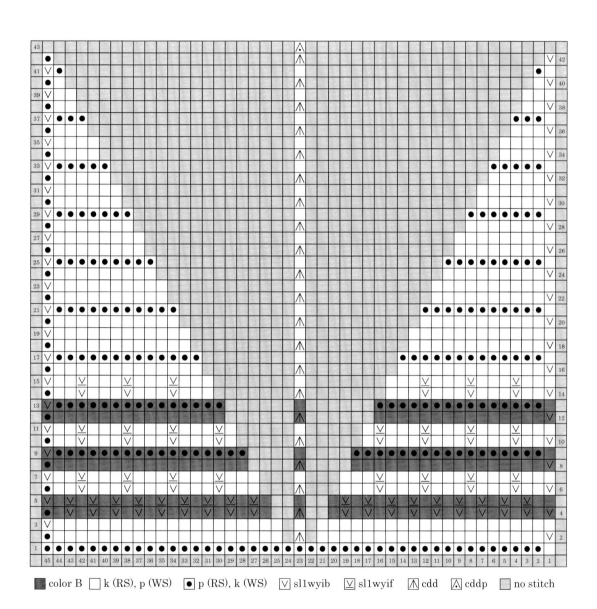

color B ☐ k (RS), p (WS) ● p (RS), k (WS) ☑ sl1wyib ☑ sl1wyif ⋀ cdd ⋀ cddp ☐ no stitch

Color Square 16

Adaptability 2 Increase or decrease by a multiple of 12 stitches.

Color Square 16

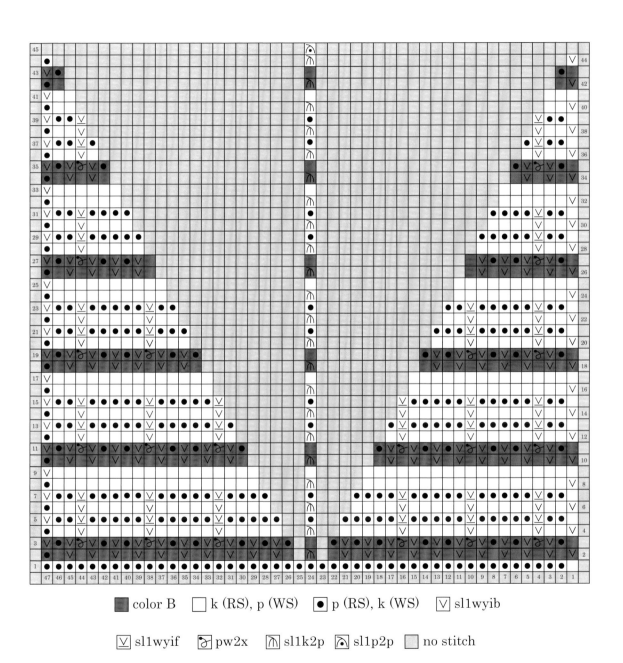

	color B		k (RS), p (WS)		p (RS), k (WS)	☑ sl1wyib

☑ sl1wyif   ⟲ pw2x   ⋀ sl1k2p   ⟑ sl1p2p   ☐ no stitch

Texture Square 17

Adaptability I Any odd number of stitches can be used.

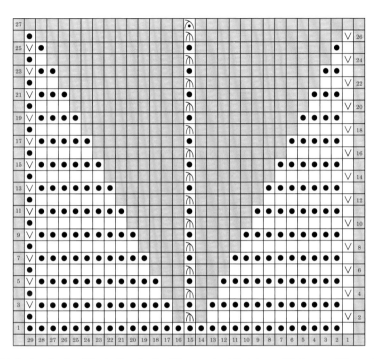

☐ k (RS), p (WS) ● p (RS), k (WS) ∨ sl1wyib ⼧ sl1k2p ⼧ sl1p2p ☐ no stitch

Texture Square 18

Adaptability 2 Increase or decrease by a multiple of 4 stitches.

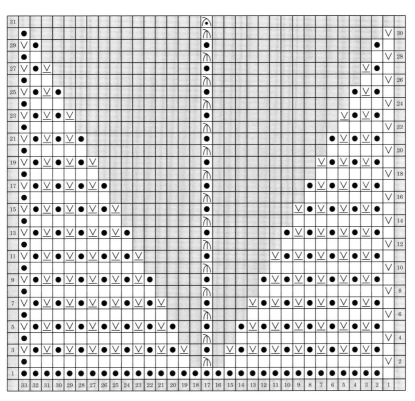

k (RS), p (WS)   ● p (RS), k (WS) $\boxed{\vee}$ sl1wyib $\boxed{\underline{\vee}}$ sl1wyif $\boxed{⅄}$ sl1k2p $\boxed{⌒}$ sl1p2p   no stitch

Texture Square 19

Adaptability 3 Best to follow chart exactly.

Texture Square 19

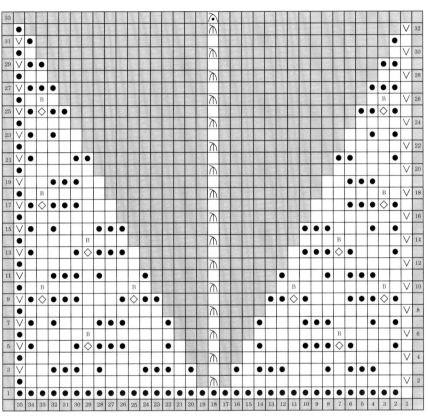

☐ k (RS), p (WS)   ● p (RS), k (WS)   ⋁ sl1wyib   ◇ bobble   Ⓑ ktbl   ⋀ sl1k2p   ⋀̇ sl1p2p   ▨ no stitch

Texture Square 20

Adaptability | Any odd number of stitches can be used. Stop stockinette stitch when there are 2 purl stitches between center decrease and stockinette stitches as in Row 15.

Texture Square 20

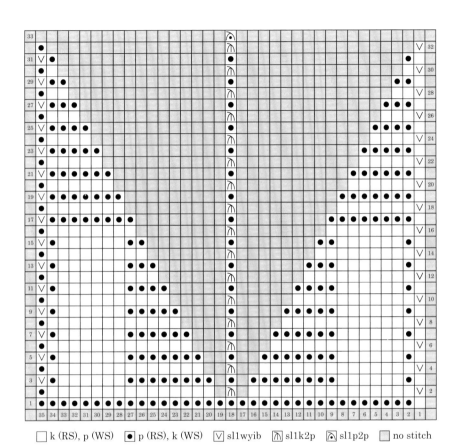

| | k (RS), p (WS) | ● p (RS), k (WS) | ∨ sl1wyib | ⩕ sl1k2p | ⩓ sl1p2p | | no stitch |

Texture Square 21

Adaptability I Any odd number of stitches can be used. Stop garter stitch when there are 2 knit stitches between center decrease and garter stitches as in Row 15.

Texture Square 21

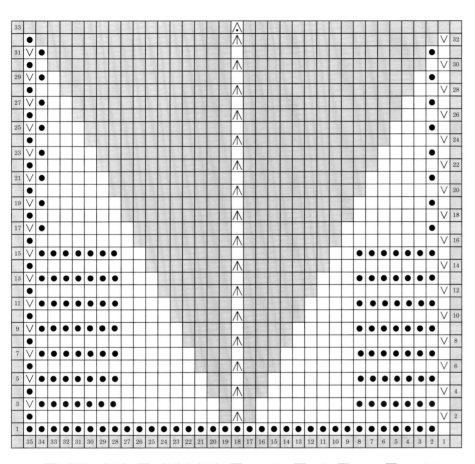

| | k (RS), p (WS) | ● | p (RS), k (WS) | ⋁ | sl1wyib | ⋀ | cdd | ⋀ | cddp | | no stitch |

Texture Square 22

Adaptability I Any odd number of stitches can be used.

Texture Square 22

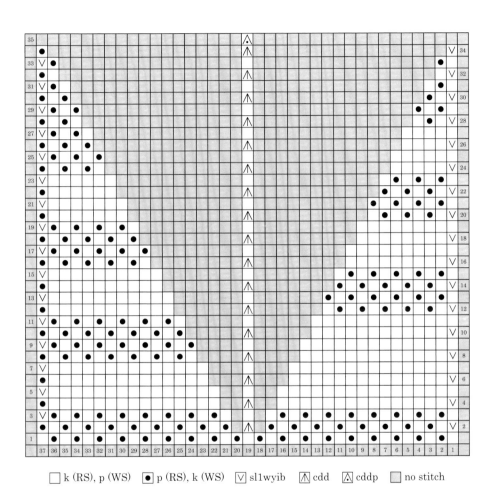

k (RS), p (WS)　　● p (RS), k (WS)　　⋁ sl1wyib　　⋀ cdd　　⋀ cddp　　no stitch

Texture Square 23

Adaptability 1 Any odd number of stitches can be used.

Texture Square 23

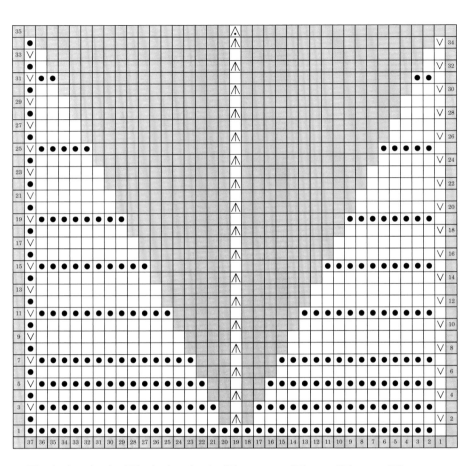

☐ k (RS), p (WS)   ● p (RS), k (WS)   ⊻ sl1wyib   ⋀ cdd   ⋀ cddp   ▨ no stitch

Texture Square 24

Adaptability 2 Increase or decrease by a multiple of 10 stitches.

Texture Square 24

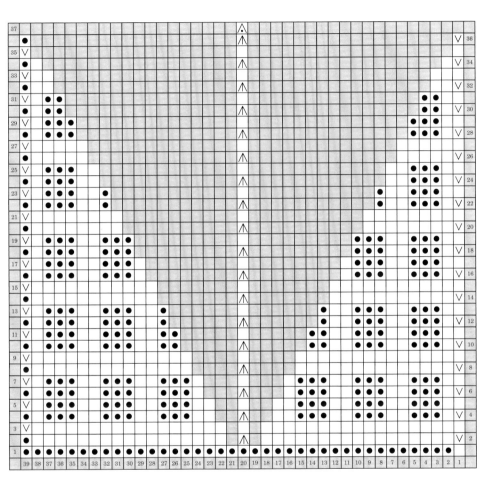

□ k (RS), p (WS)   ● p (RS), k (WS)   ∨ sl1wyib   ∧ cdd   ∧ cddp   ▨ no stitch

Texture Square 25

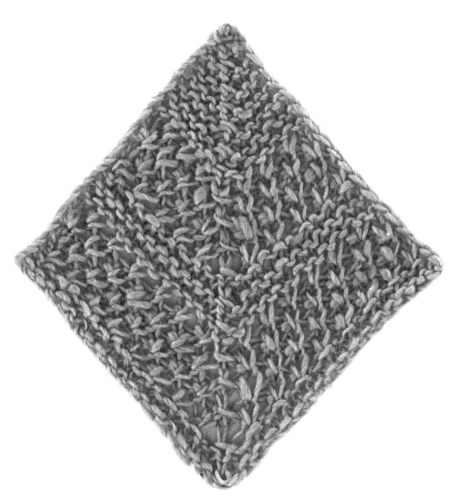

Adaptability 2 Increase or decrease by a multiple of 4 stitches.

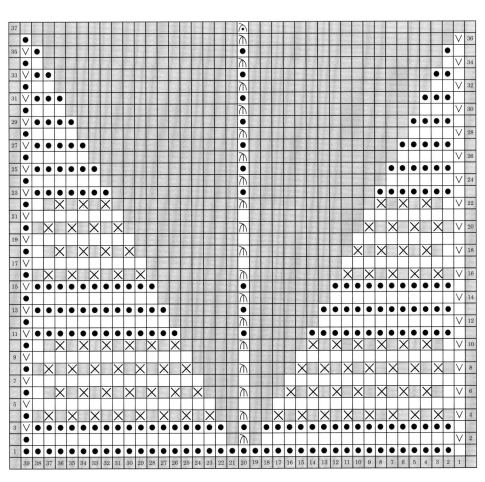

☐ k (RS), p (WS)   ⦿ p (RS), k (WS)   ∨ sl1wyib   ⊠ 2kfb   ⋀ sl1k2p   ⋀ sl1p2p   ▨ no stitch

Texture Square 26

Adaptability 3 Best to follow chart exactly.

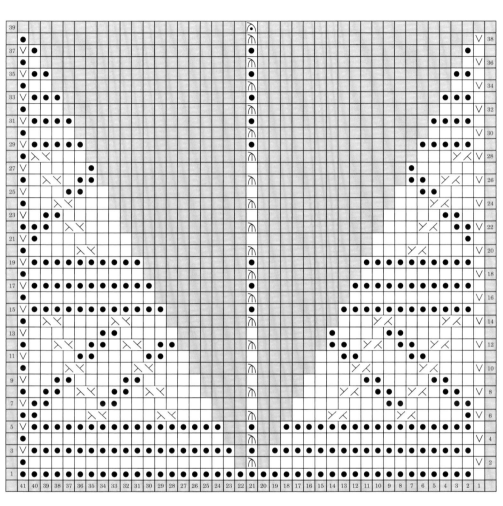

□ k (RS), p (WS)   ● p (RS), k (WS)   ⤬ lt   ⤬ rt   Ⅴ sl1wyib   ⤒ sl1k2p   ⤓ sl1p2p   ▨ no stitch

Texture Square 27

Adaptability 2 Increase or decrease by a multiple of 12 stitches.

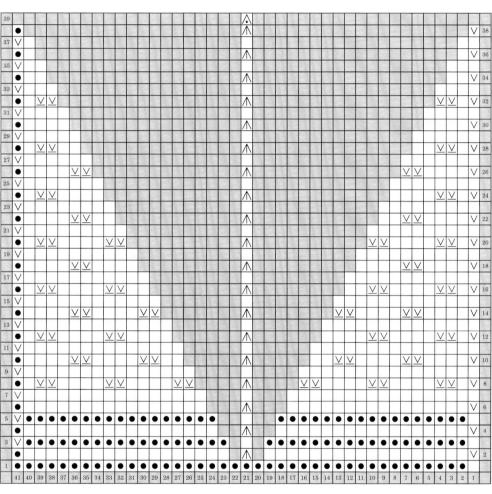

☐ k (RS), p (WS)   ● p (RS), k (WS)   ⟍V⟋ sl1wyib   ⟍V⟋ sl1wyif   ⟍∧⟋ cdd   ⟍∧⟋ cddp   ▨ no stitch

Texture Square 28

Adaptability 3 Best to follow chart exactly.

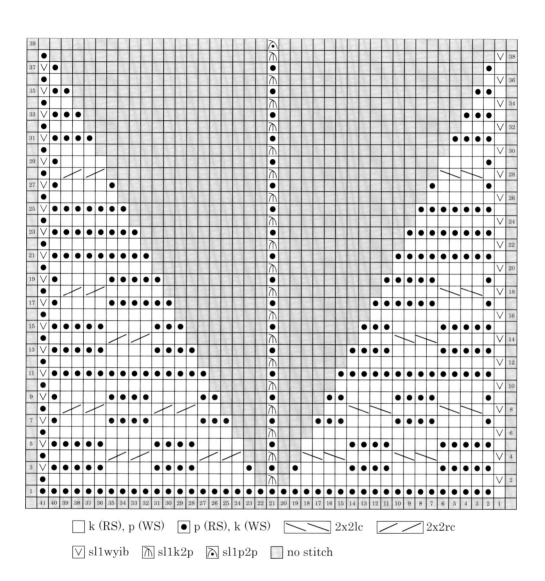

| | k (RS), p (WS) | ● p (RS), k (WS) | ╲ 2x2lc | ╱ 2x2rc |

| ∨ sl1wyib | ⋔ sl1k2p | ⌂ sl1p2p | no stitch |

Texture Square 29

Adaptability 2 Increase or decrease by a multiple of 8 stitches.

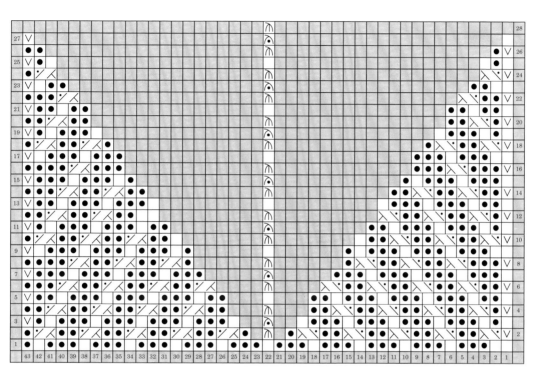

☐ k (RS), p (WS) ● p (RS), k (WS) ⟋⟍ 1x1lpc ⟋⟍ 1x1rpc ⋁ sl1wyib ⟰ sl1k2p ⟰ sl1p2p ☐ no stitch

Texture Square 30

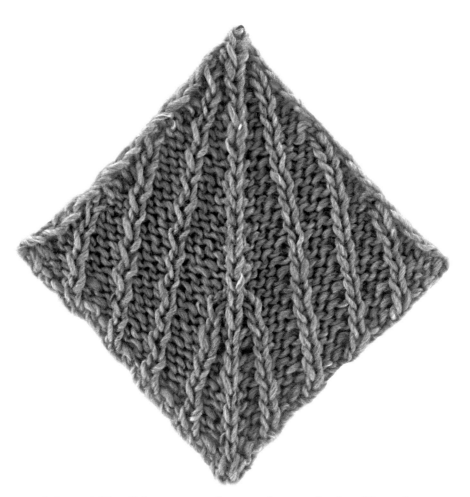

Adaptability 2 Increase or decrease by a multiple of 8 stitches.

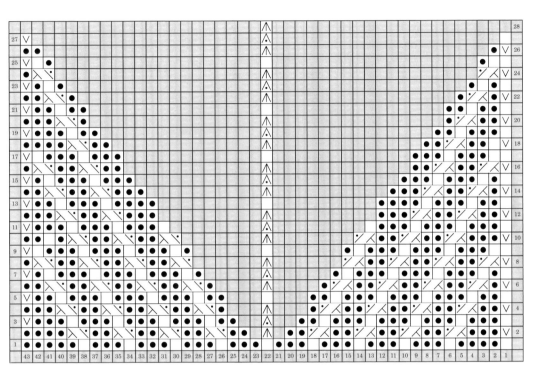

| | k (RS), p (WS) | ● | p (RS), k (WS) | ⟍⟍ | 1x1lpc | ⟋⟋ | 1x1rpc | V | sl1wyib | ⋀ | cdd | ⋀ | cddp | | no stitch |

Lace Square 31

Adaptability 1 Any odd number of stitches can be used.

Lace Square 31

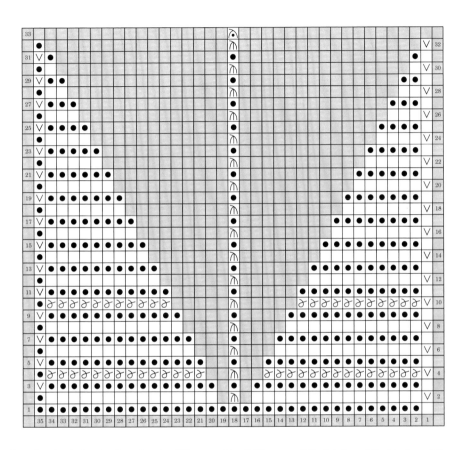

$\square$ k (RS), p (WS)　$\boxed{\bullet}$ p (RS), k (WS)　$\boxed{\vee}$ sl1wyib　$\boxed{\partial}$ kw2x　$\boxed{\wedge}$ sl1k2p　$\boxed{\wedge}$ sl1p2p　$\boxed{}$ no stitch

Lace Square 32

Adaptability 3 Best to follow chart exactly.

Lace Square 32

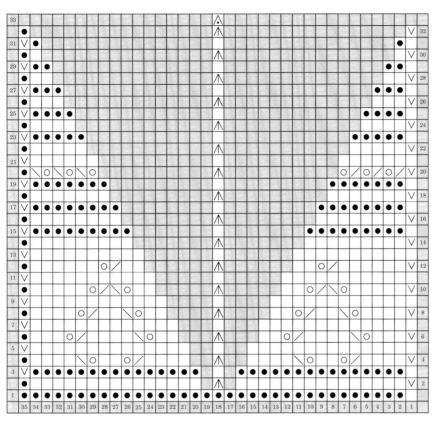

| | k (RS), p (WS) | ● | p (RS), k (WS) | ∨ | sl1wyib | ○ | yo | ╱ | k2tog | ╲ | ssk | ⋀ | cdd | ⋀ | cddp | | no stitch |

Lace Square 33

Adaptability 2 Increase or decrease by a multiple of 4 stitches. Stop lace when there are 2 purl stitches between center decrease and lace as in Row 16.

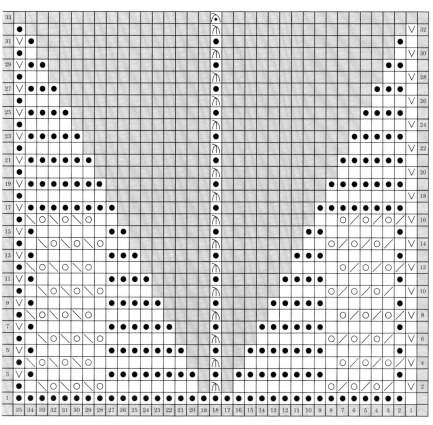

k (RS), p (WS)   ● p (RS), k (WS)   ∨ sl1wyib   ○ yo   ╱ k2tog   ╲ ssk   ⋀ sl1k2p   sl1p2p   no stitch

Lace Square 34

Adaptability I Any odd number of stitches can be used.

Lace Square 34

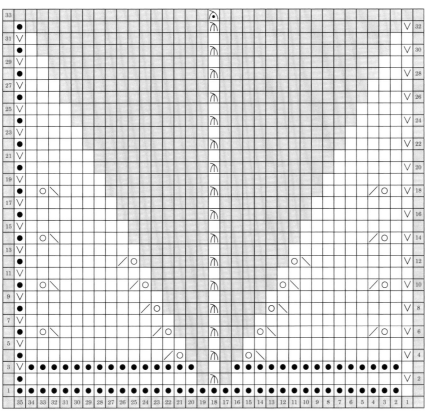

| | | k (RS), p (WS) | ● | p (RS), k (WS) | ∨ | sl1wyib | ○ | yo | ╱ | k2tog | ╲ | ssk | ⋔ | sl1k2p | ⋔ | sl1p2p | | no stitch |

Lace Square 35

Adaptability 2 Increase or decrease by a multiple of 4 stitches. Stop garter stitch when there are 2 stockinette stitches between center decrease and garter stitches as in Row 15.

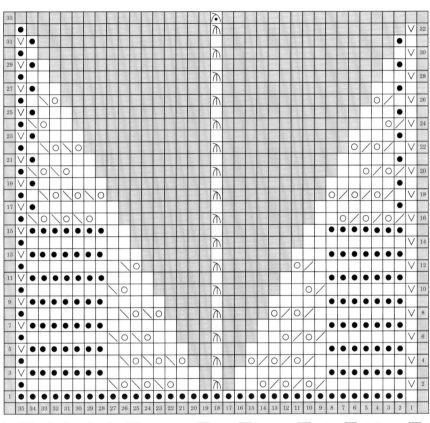

| | k (RS), p (WS) | ● | p (RS), k (WS) | ∨ | sl1wyib | ○ | yo | ╱ | k2tog | ╲ | ssk | ⌐⌐ | sl1k2p | ● | sl1p2p | | no stitch |

Lace Square 36

Adaptability 2 Increase or decrease by a multiple of 4 stitches.

Lace Square 36

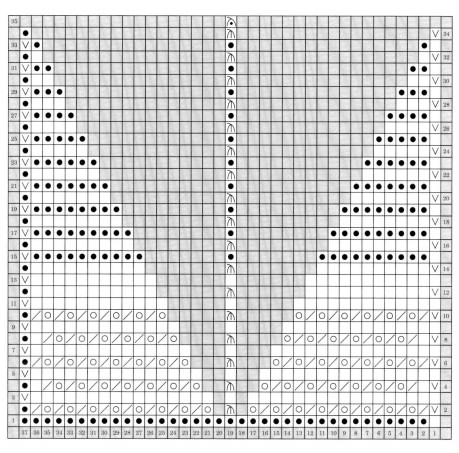

| | k (RS), p (WS) | ● p (RS), k (WS) | ∨ sl1wyib | ○ yo | ╱ k2tog | 🡑 sl1k2p | 🡑 sl1p2p | | no stitch |

Lace Square 37

Adaptability 2 Increase or decrease by a multiple of 4 stitches.

Lace Square 37

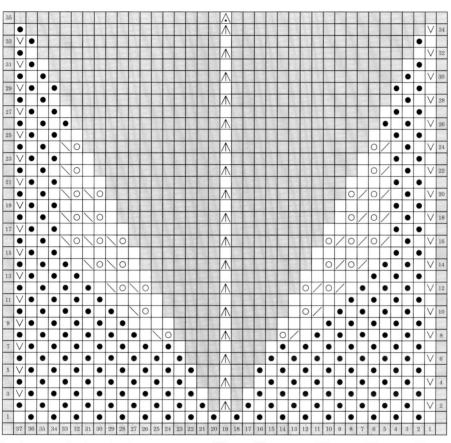

☐ k (RS), p (WS)   ● p (RS), k (WS)   ⋁ sl1wyib   ○ yo   ╱ k2tog   ╲ ssk   ⋀ cdd   ⋀̇ cddp   ▨ no stitch

Lace Square 38

Adaptability 2 Increase or decrease by a multiple of 4 stitches.

Lace Square 38

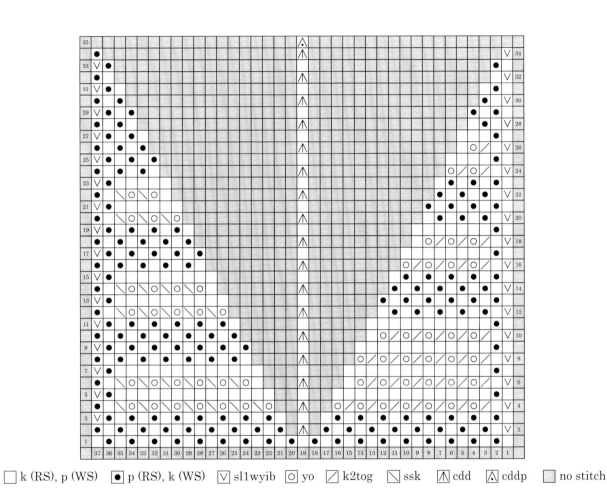

☐ k (RS), p (WS)　● p (RS), k (WS)　☑ sl1wyib　◯ yo　⟋ k2tog　⟍ ssk　⋀ cdd　⟁ cddp　▨ no stitch

Lace Square 39

Adaptability 2 Increase or decrease by a multiple of 4 stitches.

Lace Square 39

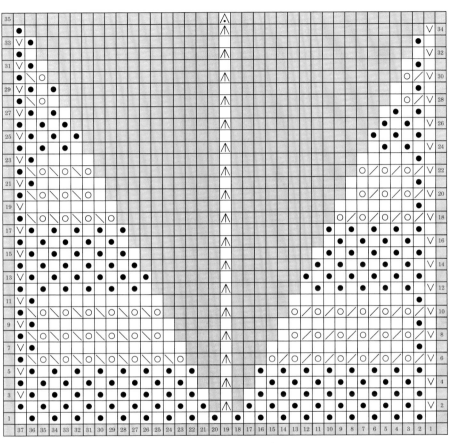

| | k (RS), p (WS) | ● | p (RS), k (WS) | V | sl1wyib | O | yo | ⟋ | k2tog | ⟍ | ssk | ⋀ | cdd | ⋀ | cddp | | no stitch |

Lace Square 40

Adaptability 2 Increase or decrease by a multiple of 4 stitches.

Lace Square 40

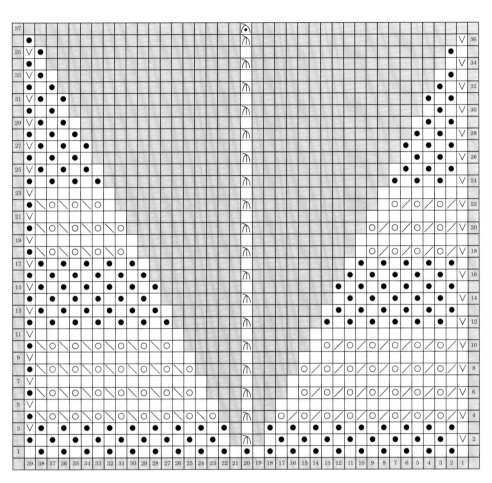

| | k (RS), p (WS) | ● p (RS), k (WS) | ∨ sl1wyib | ○ yo | ╱ k2tog | ╲ ssk | ⚇ sl1k2p | ⊙ sl1p2p | | no stitch |

Lace Square 41

Adaptability 3 Best to follow chart exactly.

Lace Square 41

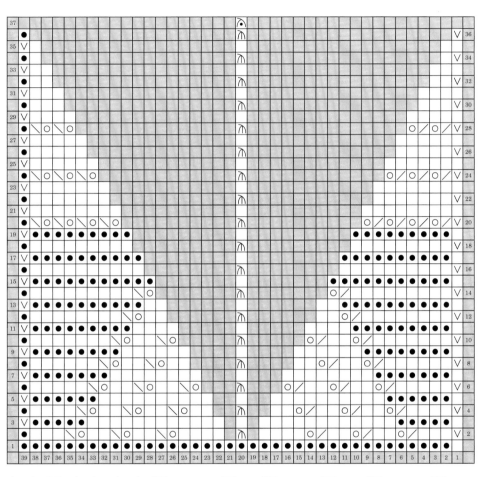

□ k (RS), p (WS)   ● p (RS), k (WS)   ⋁ sl1wyib   ○ yo   ╱ k2tog   ╲ ssk   ⋀ sl1k2p   ⟁ sl1p2p   ▦ no stitch

Lace Square 42

Adaptability 2 Increase or decrease by a multiple of 6 stitches.

Lace Square 42

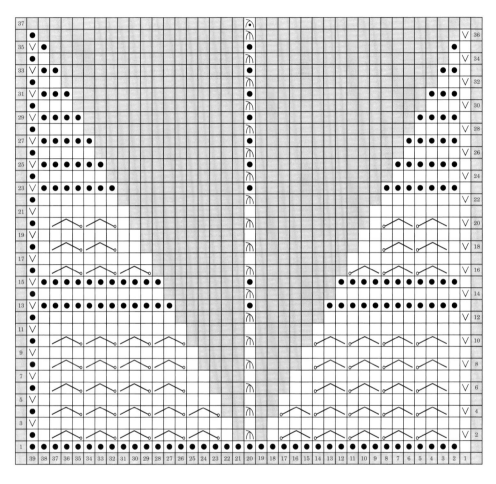

☐ k (RS), p (WS)   ● p (RS), k (WS)   Ⓥ sl1wyib   ◠ yos1k2   ◠ s1k2yo   Ⓐ sl1k2p   Ⓐ sl1p2p   ☐ no stitch

Lace Square 43

Adaptability 2 Increase or decrease by a multiple of 12 stitches.

Lace Square 43

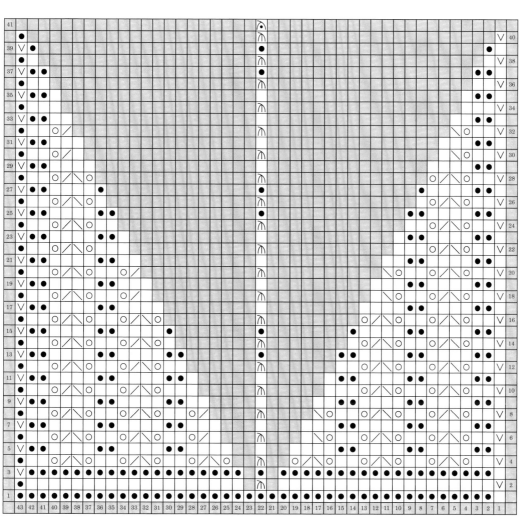

☐ k (RS), p (WS) ● p (RS), k (WS) ⩔ sl1wyib ○ yo ╱ k2tog ╲ ssk ⋀ sl1k2p ⦚ sl1p2p ☐ no stitch

Lace Square 44

Adaptability 2 Increase or decrease by a multiple of 4 stitches.

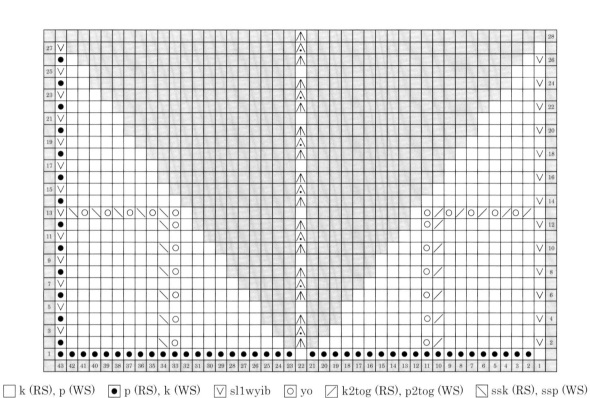

☐ k (RS), p (WS)   ● p (RS), k (WS)   ⋁ sl1wyib   ⊙ yo   ⟋ k2tog (RS), p2tog (WS)   ⟍ ssk (RS), ssp (WS)

⋀ cdd   ⋀ cddp   ☐ no stitch

Lace Square 45

Adaptability 2 Increase or decrease by a multiple of 12 stitches.

Lace Square 45

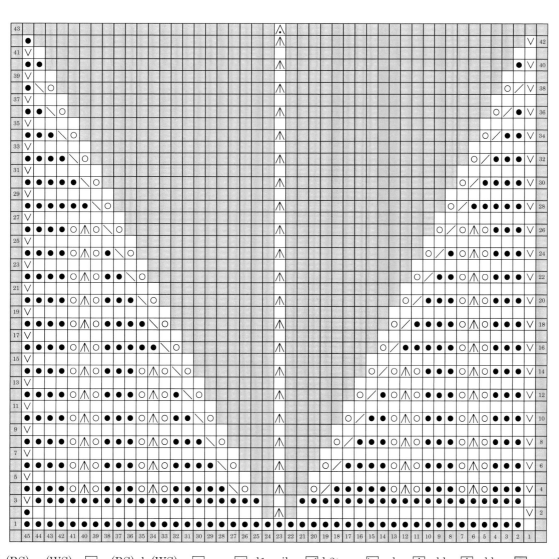

☐ k (RS), p (WS) ● p (RS), k (WS) ○ yo ⋁ sl1wyib ╱ k2tog ╲ ssk ⋀ cdd ⋀ cddp ▨ no stitch

Frosty
Sunrise

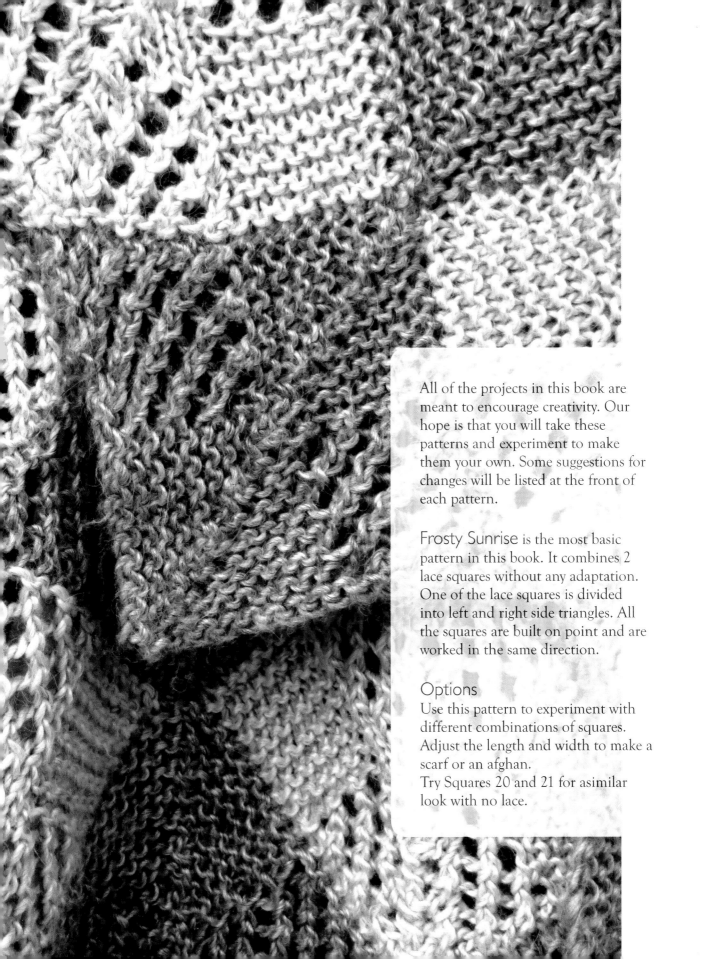

All of the projects in this book are meant to encourage creativity. Our hope is that you will take these patterns and experiment to make them your own. Some suggestions for changes will be listed at the front of each pattern.

Frosty Sunrise is the most basic pattern in this book. It combines 2 lace squares without any adaptation. One of the lace squares is divided into left and right side triangles. All the squares are built on point and are worked in the same direction.

Options
Use this pattern to experiment with different combinations of squares. Adjust the length and width to make a scarf or an afghan.
Try Squares 20 and 21 for asimilar look with no lace.

Frosty Sunrise

Materials

DK–weight alpaca or alpaca–blend yarn, 588 yards each of 2 colors. Sample is knit with **Blue Sky Alpacas** *Metalico* in Platinum (A–grey squares in schematic) and Silver (B–white squares in schematic).

Needles

US 5 (3.75mm) 16" circular needle, size F crochet hook (optional).

Gauge

Square measures 4.5" point to point.

Finished Measurements

14" X 54 (63)".

Notes

Left and Right Triangle charts can be found on pg. 125.

Set Up

Square 1, 2, 3, Color A

Cast on 35 stitches.
Work Lace Square 33 (pg. 76),
leaving last stitch live on a locking stitch marker.

Triangle 4, Color B

Work right side triangle,
leaving last stitch live on a locking stitch marker.

103

Frosty Sunrise

Square 5, 6, Color B

Pu&k 17 along left side of Square 1, insert needle into left corner of first square and right corner of second square and connect by pu&k 1 corner stitch through both points, then pu&k 17 along right side of second square.

Work Lace Square 35 (pg. 80)
leaving last stitch live on a locking stitch marker.

Triangle 7, Color B

Work left side triangle,
leaving last stitch live on a locking stitch marker.

Squares 8, 9, 10, Color A

Pu&k as for Square 5, knitting live stitch from square below as center stitch.
Work Lace Square 33 (pg. 76)
leaving last stitch live on a locking stitch marker.

Continue working squares and triangles following schematic on this page. For longer version, repeat Squares 67-80.

Fasten off last stitch on Squares 78, 79 and 80 for short version or squares 91, 92 and 93 for longer version.

Finishing

Block. Work single crochet along left and right side triangles (optional).

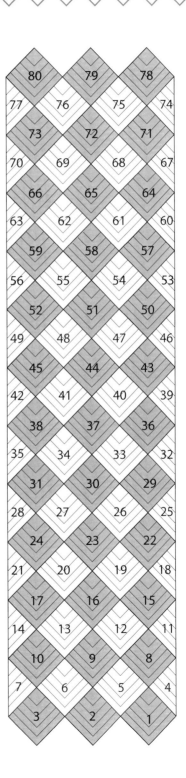

Harvest
Celebration

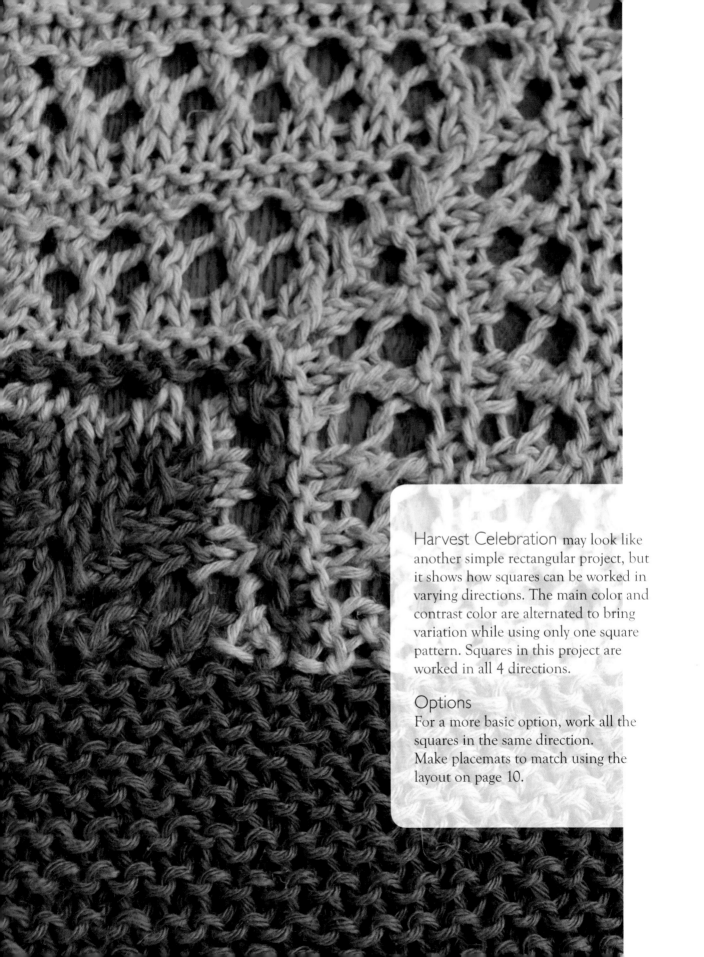

Harvest Celebration may look like
another simple rectangular project, but
it shows how squares can be worked in
varying directions. The main color and
contrast color are alternated to bring
variation while using only one square
pattern. Squares in this project are
worked in all 4 directions.

Options
For a more basic option, work all the
squares in the same direction.
Make placemats to match using the
layout on page 10.

Harvest Celebration

Materials
DK-weight hemp or linen yarn, 280 yards A, 140 yards B.
Sample is knit with **Lanaknits** *AllHemp 6* in Deep Sea (A) and Sprout (B).

Needles
US 6 (4mm) 24" circular needle and 1 set of short straight needles.

Gauge
Square measures 5.5" side to side.

Finished Measurements
15" X 37"

Set Up

Squares 1, 2
With Color B, cast on 43 stitches.
Work Color Square 14 (pg. 38).
Fasten off last stitch.

Square 3
With Color A, pu&k 21 stitches along right side of Square 1, insert needle into the point of each square and connect by pu&k 1 center stitch through both points, then pu&k 21 stitches along bottom edge of Square 2. Work square, leaving last stitch live on a locking stitch marker.

Square 4
With Color A, pu&k 21 stitches along left side of Square 2, pu&k 1 corner stitch, then pu&k 21 stitches along top of Square 1. Work square, leaving last stitch live on a locking stitch marker.

Square 5
With Color B, cast on 21 stitches, knit live stitch of Square 4, then pu&k 21 stitches on left side of Square 4. Work square, leaving last stitch live.

Square 6
Use live stitch of Square 5 for first picked-up stitch of Square 6. With Color A, pu&k 20 more stitches across bottom of Square 5, pu&k 1 corner stitch, then pu&k 21 stitches along left side of Square 1. Work square, leaving last stitch live on a locking stitch marker.

Square 7

With Color B, pu&k 22 stitches along edge of Square 6, knitting live stitch of Square 6 for last picked-up stitch, then cast on 21 stitches. Work square, leaving last stitch live on a locking stitch marker.

Square 8

With Color A, pu&k 21 stitches along left side of Square 5, pu&k 1 corner stitch, then pu&k 21 stitches along top of Square 7, knitting live stitch of Square 7 for last picked-up stitch. Work square, fastening off last stitch.

Square 9

Work as for Square 5, onto Square 3.

Square 10

Work as for Square 6, onto Squares 9 and 2, knitting live stitch of Square 9 for first picked-up stitch of Square 10.

Square 11

Work as for Square 7, onto Square 10.

Square 12

Work as for Square 8, onto Squares 9 and 11, knitting live stitch of Square 11 for last picked-up stitch of Square 12.

Borders

Top and bottom borders

With RS facing and using Color A, pu&k 126 stitches along long edges. Work 9 ridges of garter stitch, ending with a WS row. Bind off loosely.

Side borders

With RS facing and using Color A, pu&k 42 stitches along short edges. Work 9 ridges of garter stitch, ending with a WS row. Bind off loosely.

Corner squares

Using Color B, pu&k 10 stitches along edge of one border, pu&k 1 corner stitch, then pu&k 10 stitches along edge of second border. Complete square.

Finishing

Block by handwashing and laying flat to dry, for best shape retention.

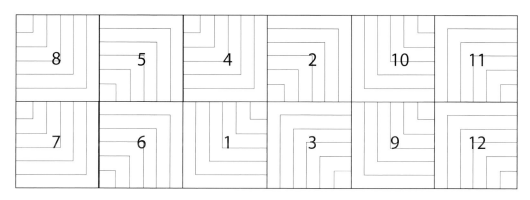

Misty Valley

Designing with mitered squares creates some restrictions in the armhole and shoulder sizing. Misty Valley shows a simple way to add mitered squares and avoid those challenging areas. Adding mitered squares to just the front edge only restricts the length. Notice that the last 3 sizes are longer than the first 2 sizes due to the addition of one more row of squares.

Options

This pattern makes it easy to swap lengths. Want the length other than the one written for your size? Pu&k 110 stitches for the short length and 132 for the long length. Follow the remaining instructions for your size.

Try using Square 24. It shows a different stitch pattern on the front and back.

Misty Valley

Materials

Fine-weight linen or linen-blend yarn, 900 (990, 1050, 1120, 1200) yards.
Sample is knit with **Fiesta Yarns** *Linnette* in Ancient Ruins.

Needles

US 4 (3.5mm) 24" circular needle, US 4 (3.5mm) double-pointed needles (optional).

Gauge

Square measures 3.25" side to side. 27 stitches and 34 rows over 4" in stockinette stitch.

Finished Measurements

36 (40, 44, 48, 52)"

Notes

Squares 3a, 8a, 15a, and 16a in schematic are for extra length for 3 largest sizes. Do not work if making 36" or 40" size.

Left Side Squares

Square 1
Cast on 35 stitches.
Work Lace Square 31 (pg. 72),
leaving last stitch live on a locking stitch marker.

Square 2
Starting at left of live stitch with RS facing, pu&k 18 stitches, then cast on 17 stitches.
Work Lace Square 31 (pg. 72),
leaving last stitch live on a locking stitch marker.

Squares 3, 4, 5
Work as for Square 2.

Square 6
Cast on 17 stitches, then pu&k 18 stitches from Square 1.
Work Lace Square 31 (pg. 72).
Fasten off last stitch.

Square 7
With RS facing, pu&k 17 stitches along top of Square 6, knit live stitch from Square 1, then pu&k 17 stitches from Square 2.
Work Lace Square 31 (pg. 72).
Fasten off last stitch.

Square 8, 9, 10
Work as for Square 7.

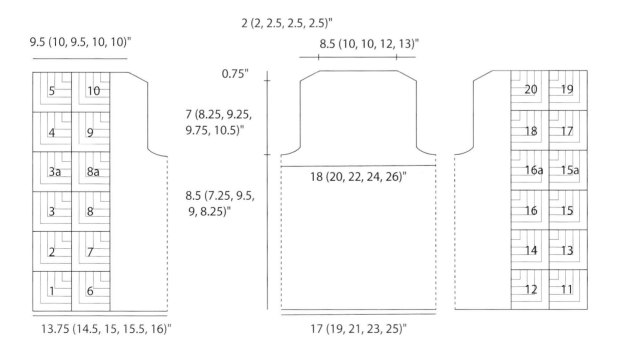

Misty Valley

Left Side Body

With RS facing and starting at right edge of Left Side Squares, pu&k 110 (110, 132, 132, 132) stitches. (WS) Sl1, purl to last 4 stitches, k4. (RS) Sl1, knit to end. Work in stockinette stitch with 4 stitches of bottom edge in garter stitch until piece measures 9.5 (10, 9.5, 10, 10)", ending with a WS row.

Shoulder decrease

Dec row (RS) Work to last 4 stitches, k2tog, k1, p1. Repeat Dec row every 4th row 4 (4, 5, 5, 5) times-105 (105, 126, 126, 126) stitches.

Armhole decrease

(WS) Bind off 37 (41, 44, 47, 51) stitches, work to end-68 (64, 82, 79, 75) stitches. [Dec row (RS) Work to last 4 stitches, k2tog, k1, p1. (WS) Bind off 2 (3, 4, 4, 5) stitches, work to end] 3 times. Repeat Dec row every other

row 1 (3, 2, 3, 1) times, then every 4th row 1 (0, 1, 0, 1) time-57 (49, 64, 61, 55) stitches. Work even for 7 (9, 11, 13, 17) rows ending with a WS row. Use waste yarn or a locking stitch marker at beginning and end of row to mark side 'seam'. Work 6 (8, 10, 12, 16) rows even.

Armhole increase

Inc row (RS) Work to last 2 stitches, ML, k1, p1. Repeat Inc row every 4th row 1 (0, 1, 0, 1) time, then every other row 1 (3, 2, 3, 1) times. [(WS) Cast on 2 (3, 4, 4, 5) stitches, work to end. (RS) Work Inc row.] twice, then work WS row once more. Work 1 row even. Cast on 37 (41, 44, 47, 51) stitches-105 (105, 126, 126, 126) stitches. (WS) Work 1 row even.

Shoulder increase

Inc row (RS) Work to last 2 stitches, ML, k1, p1. Repeat Inc row every 4th row 4 (4, 5, 5, 5) times-110 (110, 132, 132, 132) stitches. Work even until piece measures 8.5 (9.5, 10.5, 11.5, 12.5)" from side 'seam' markers, ending with a RS row. (WS) Sl1, p53, w&t. (RS) Sl1, k52 wrapping yarn 2 times around each stitch, p1. (WS) Sl1, purl to end, dropping all extra wraps. Place all stitches on waste yarn.

Right Side Squares

Squares 11, 12

Work as for Squares 1 and 2, leaving last stitch of Square 11 live and fasten off last stitch of Square 12.

Square 13

Cast on 17 stitches. With RS facing, starting at

top right of square below, pu&k 18 stitches. *Work Square 31 (pg. 72),* leaving last stitch live on a locking stitch marker.

Squares 14, 16, 18

Work as for Square 7.

Squares 15, 17, 19

Work as for Square 13.

Square 20

Start with live stitch of Square 19 when picking up stitches. Work as for Square 7, leaving last stitch live.

Right Side Body

With RS facing and starting with live stitch of Square 20, pu&k 110 (110, 132, 132, 132) stitches. (WS) Sl1, k3, purl to end. (RS) Sl1, knit to end. Work in stockinette stitch with 4 stitches of bottom edge in garter stitch until piece measures 9.5 (10, 9.5, 10, 10)", ending with a WS row.

Shoulder decrease

Dec row (RS) Sl1, k1, ssk, work to end. Repeat Dec row every 4th row 4 (4, 5, 5, 5) times-105 (105, 126, 126, 126) stitches. Work 1 row even.

Armhole decrease

(RS) Bind off 37 (41, 44, 47, 51) stitches, work to end-68 (64, 82, 79, 75) stitches. Work 1 row even. [Dec row (RS) Bind off 2 (3, 4, 4, 5) stitches, k1, ssk, work to end. (WS) Work 1 row even.] 3 times. Repeat Inc row every other row

1 (3, 2, 3, 1) times, then every 4th row 1 (0, 1, 0, 1) time-57, 49, 64, 61, 55) stitches. Work even for 7 (9, 11, 13, 17) rows, ending with a WS row). Use waste yarn or a locking stitch marker at beginning and end of row to mark side 'seam'. Work 6 (8, 10, 12, 16) rows even.

Armhole increase

Inc row (RS) Sl1, k1, MR, work to end. Repeat Inc row every 4th row 1 (0, 1, 0, 1) time, then every other row 1 (3, 2, 3, 1) times. [Cast-on Row (WS) Work to end, cast on 2 (3, 4, 4, 5) stitches. (RS) K3 (4, 5, 5, 6), MR, work to end.] twice, then work Cast-on Row once more-68 (64, 82, 79, 75) stitches. Work 1 row even. (WS) Work to end, cast on 37 (41, 44, 47, 51) stitches-105 (105, 126, 126, 126) stitches. Work 2 rows even.

Shoulder increase

Inc row (RS) Sl1, k1, MR, work to end. Repeat Inc row every 4th row 4 (4, 5, 5, 5) times-110 (110, 132, 132, 132) stitches. Work even until piece measures 8.5 (9.5, 10.5, 11.5, 12.5)" from side 'seam' markers, ending with a WS row. (RS) Sl1, k53 wrapping yarn 2 times around each stitch, w&t. (WS) Sl1, purl to end, dropping all extra wraps. (RS) Sl1, knit to end. Place all stitches on waste yarn.

Finishing

Sew shoulder seams together. Join left and right sides together using 3-needle bind-off. Using the 16" needle, pu&k stitches around armhole. Place marker and join to work in the round. Purl 1 round, knit 1 round, purl 1 round. Bind off. Repeat for second armhole.

Aurora Night is an all-mitered-square vest. Two yarns are used in complementary colorways. The diagonal building of the squares highlights the long color changes in the yarn.
Sizing is accomplished by adapting Color Square 9 to various sizes.

Options

Swap out this square for another, change yarn weights and needle sizes - just find a square size that fits into the sizes in the pattern and create something truly unique.

Aurora Night

Materials

Fingering-weight wool yarn and lace-weight mohair, 470 (530, 590, 660, 730) yards each of 2 colors.

Purple sample is knit with **Twisted Fiber Arts** *Kabam* in Dusk (A) and **Trendsetter** *Kid Set* in Purple (B). Green sample is knit with **Yarn Hollow** *Chime* in Teal on Teal (A) and **K1C2** *Ty-Dy Superkid* in Oceana (B).

Needles

US 4 (3.5mm) double-pointed and 32" circular needles.

Gauge

Squares are measured point to point. 27 stitch = 4", 31 stitch = 4.5", 35 stitch = 5", 39 stitch = 5.5", 43 stitch = 6" Be sure to wash and block swatch before measuring.

Finished Measurements

32 (36, 40, 44, 48)"

Notes

Use 27-stitch chart for size 32", 31-stitch chart for size 36", 35-stitch chart for size 40", 39-stitch chart for size 44" and 43-stitch chart for size 48". Adapted Squares charts can be found on pgs. 120-123.

Aurora Night

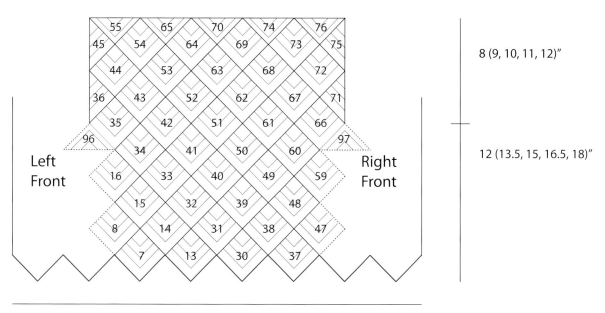

8 (9, 10, 11, 12)"

12 (13.5, 15, 16.5, 18)"

Left Front

Right Front

32 (36, 40, 44, 48)"

— Picot Cast On   — Cable Cast On

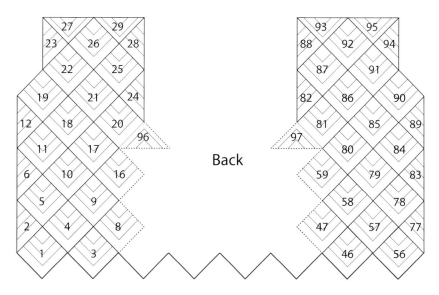

Back

Color Square Charts

27-stitch pg. 120

31-stitch pg. 121

35-stitch pg 28

39-stitch pg. 122

43-stitch pg 123

Note: work last 2 rows in both A and B.

Aurora Night

Left Front

Squares 1, 3, 7, 13, 30, 37, 46, 56
Picot Cast-on

With Color A cast on 3 stitches, bind off 2. [Do not turn. Transfer stitch from right-hand needle to left-hand needle (LH ndl). Cable cast on 3 stitches, bind off 2.] until there are 14 (16, 18, 20, 22) stitches on LH ndl. [K1, pu&k 1 in space before next stitch] to last stitch, k1, pu&k 1 at end of row 28 (32, 36, 40, 44) stitches. Row 1 (replaces row 1 of chart): K13 (15, 17, 19, 21), k2tog, k12 (14, 16, 18, 20), p1. *Work Color Square 9 (pg.28, 120-123). Begin chart with row 2.*

Work squares and triangles in order following schematic. Squares are worked diagonally to avoid breaking yarn after each square. Leave last stitch of each square live and place on a locking stitch marker.

Squares 35, 81

Pu&k 13 (15, 17, 19, 21) stitches along Squares 34 and 80, pu&k live stitch from Squares 16 and 59, then cable cast on 13 (15, 17, 19, 21) stitches.

Squares 20, 66

Cable cast on 14 (16, 18, 20, 22) stitches, pu&k 13 (15, 17, 19, 21) stitches along Squares 17 and 60.

Triangles 96, 97

Work a top triangle at underarm to close underarm seam. Fasten off last stitch.

Front Shoulders

With RS facing and using Color A and B, pu&k 33 (37, 41, 45, 49) stitches along top edge of front. Row 1 (WS): Knit. Rows 2, 3: With Color A, knit. Rows 4, 5: With Color B, knit. Row 6: With Color A and B, knit. Place stitches on hold.

Right Back Shoulder

With RS facing and using Color A and B, pu&k 33 (37, 41, 45, 49) stitches along top edge of Triangles 76 and 74. Work as for Front Shoulders through Row 6. Row 7: With Color A and B, knit. Place stitches on hold.

Left Back Shoulder

With RS facing and using Color A and B, pu&k 33 (37, 41, 45, 49) stitches along top edge of Triangles 65 and 55. Work as for Front Shoulders through Row 6. Row 7: With Color A and B, knit. Place stitches on hold.

Finishing

Join shoulder seams using a 3-needle bind-off with WS facing out. To strengthen this seam, work 1 row of back stitch on the WS, across bottom of bind-off seam.

Neckband

The neckband is worked in one piece. As live stitches from squares are reached, knit them into pick-up row of neckband. Using the 32" circular needle, with RS facing and Color A, beginning at bottom edge, pu&k an odd number of stitches along right front edge to beginning of angled edge, knit live stitch at corner and mark, pu&k an even number of

27-Stitch Chart

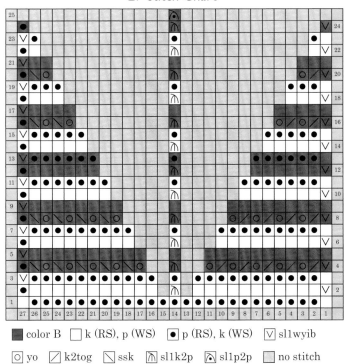

color B ☐ k (RS), p (WS) ● p (RS), k (WS) ⊻ sl1wyib

☐ yo ╱ k2tog ╲ ssk ⋔ sl1k2p ⋔ sl1p2p ☐ no stitch

Aurora Night Charts

31-Stitch Chart

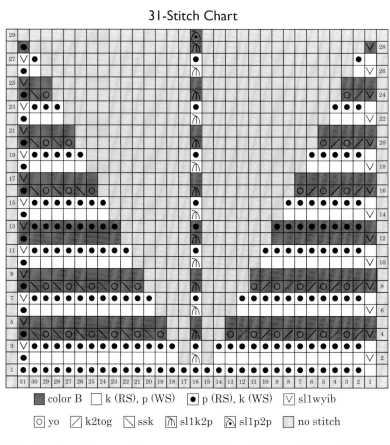

color B ☐ k (RS), p (WS) ● p (RS), k (WS) ⊻ sl1wyib

○ yo ╱ k2tog ⧹ ssk ⋔ sl1k2p ⋔ sl1p2p ☐ no stitch

stitches along angled edge, knit live stitch in corner and mark, pu&k an even number of stitches from top of angled edge to top of angled edge on opposite side. Pu&k the same number of stitches from here to bottom edge, marking 2 corner stitches as on first side.

Row 1 (WS): With Color A, sl1, [knit to marked stitch, p1] 4 times, knit to last stitch, p1.

Row 2: With Color B, sl1, [yo, k2tog] to marked stitch, yo, k1 (marked stitch), yo, [k2tog, yo] to 2 stitches before marked stitch, k1, cdd, [k2tog, yo] to 1 stitch before marked stitch, cdd, k1, [yo, k2tog] to marked stitch, yo,

k1(marked stitch), yo, [k2tog, yo] to last stitch, p1.

Row 3: With Color B, sl1, purl to end.

Row 4: With Color A, sl1, knit to marked stitch, yo, k1 (marked stitch), yo, knit to 1 stitch before marked stitch, cdd, knit to 1 stitch before marker decreasing 4 stitches evenly spaced, cdd, knit to marked stitch, yo, k1 (marked stitch), yo, knit to last stitch, p1.

Row 5: Work as Row 1 with Color A.

Row 6: Work as Row 2 with Color B.

Row 7: Work as Row 3 with Color B.

Row 8: With Color A, work as for Row 4 eliminating the decreases.

121

39-Stitch Chart

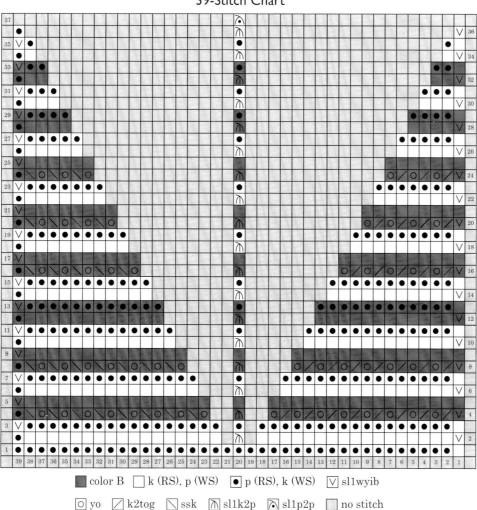

color B | | k (RS), p (WS) | | p (RS), k (WS) | | sl1wyib

yo | | k2tog | | ssk | | sl1k2p | | sl1p2p | | no stitch

Row 9: With Color A, knit.
Bind off loosely.

Armhole bands

Using the 16" circular needle and Color A, pu&k an even number of stitches around the armhole edge. PM and join to work in the round.

Rounds 1, 5 and 9: With Color A, purl.
Rounds 2 and 6: With Color B, [k2tog, yo] to end.
Rounds 3 and 7: With Color B knit.
Rounds 4 and 8: With Color A, knit.
Bind off loosely.

Aurora Night Charts

43-Stitch Chart

■ color B　□ k (RS), p (WS)　● p (RS), k (WS)　Ⅴ sl1wyib

○ yo　／ k2tog　＼ ssk　⑂ sl1k2p　⑂ sl1p2p　□ no stitch

Glossary

Definitions and Abbreviations

1x2lc - drop stitch off needle, slip 2 stitches to right needle, pick up dropped stitch with left needle, slip 2 stitches back to left needle, k3

1x1lpc - slip 1 stitch to CN, hold to front, p1, k1 from CN

1x2rc - slip 2 stitches to right needle, drop stitch off needle, move 2 stitches back to left needle, pick up dropped stitch with left needle, k3

1x1rpc - slip 1 stitch to CN, hold to back, k1, p1 from CN

2kfb - knit 2 together through front and back

2x2lc - slip 2 stitches to CN, hold to front, k2, k2 from CN

2x2rc - slip 2 stitches to CN, hold to back, k2, k2 from CN

B - ktbl - knit through back loop

be - begin next row at other end of square

bobble - (k1, yo, k1) in same stitch, [turn, p3, turn, k3] twice, pass stitches 1 and 2 over stitch 3

cdd - center double decrease - slip 2 stitches knitwise at the same time, k1, pass 2 slipped stitches over

cddp - slip 2 stitches purlwise through the back loops at the same time, p1, pass 2 slipped stitches over

CN - cable needle

k - knit

k2tog - knit 2 together

kw2x - knit, wrapping yarn around needle 2 times

lt - left twist - knit through back of second stitch, leave on needle, k2tog, slip both stitches off needle

ML - Make 1 left - Pick up and knit the loop 2 stitches below the stitch you just knit.

MR - Make 1 right - Pick up loop under the stitch on the left-hand needle and slip it onto the left-hand needle, then knit it

p - purl

p2tog - purl 2 together

pu&k - pick up and knit - insert needle into both legs of slipped stitch (or stitch from cast on edge), then knit it

pw2x - purl, wrapping yarn around needle 2 times

RS - right side

rt - right twist - k2tog leaving stitches on needle, knit through first stitch again, slip both stitches off left needle

Sl1 - Slip 1

sl1k2p - slip 1, k2tog, pass slipped stitch over

sl1p2p --slip 1, p2tog, pass slipped stitch over

Glossary

s1k2yo - slip 1, k2, pass slipped stitch over, yo

sl1wyib - slip 1 with yarn in back

sl1wyif - slip 1 with yarn in front

ssk - slip 2 stitches knitwise one at a time, slip same 2 stitches back to left needle, k2tog through back loops

ssp - with yarn in back, slip 2 stitches knitwise one at a time, slip stitches back to left needle, p2tog through back loops

w&t - wrap and turn - bring yarn from back to front if knitting, front to back if purling, between the needles. Slip next stitch as if to pur bring yarn back to original position

WS - wrong side

yo - yarn over - bring yarn over the needle fro front to back

yos1k2 - yo, slip 1, k2, pass slipped stitch over knit stitches

Frosty Sunrise Left Triangle

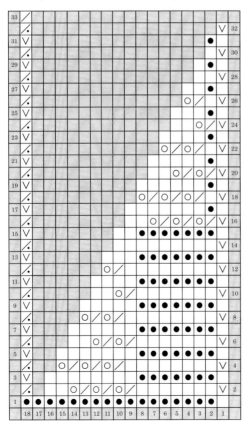

Frosty Sunrise Right Triangle

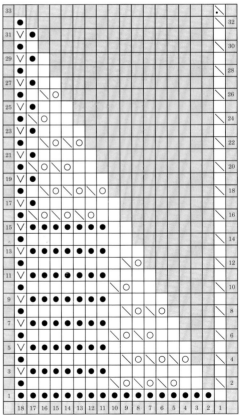

□ k (RS), p (WS)   ● p (RS), k (WS)   V sl1wyib   ○ yo   ╱ k2tog   ╲ ssk   ◣ ssp   ▨ p2tog   ▨ no sti

125